Tacking Stitch

poems by

Victoria Korth

Finishing Line Press
Georgetown, Kentucky

Tacking Stitch

Copyright © 2022 by Victoria Korth
ISBN 978-1-64662-881-0 First Edition
All rights reserved under International and Pan-American Copyright Conventions. No part of this book may be reproduced in any manner whatsoever without written permission from the publisher, except in the case of brief quotations embodied in critical articles and reviews.

ACKNOWLEDGMENTS

Thank you to the following literary magazines and anthologies in which these poems first appeared:

"parable mood" ~ *Voices Amidst the Virus,* Lily Poetry Review Books
"Horse Farm" ~ *Homestead Review*
"Thread" ~ *The Common Ground Review*
"Five Breaths" ~ *Ocean State Review*
"Tuft"~ *Le Mot Juste Anthology*
"Among Chickens" ~ *Jelly Bucket*
"Body Continuous" ~ *Stickman Review*

and to Tupelo Press 30/30 Project, March 2020 for posting early versions of the following:

"Reading Eavan Boland's 'That the Science of Cartography Is Limited'"; "Credo" formerly "Sanctuary"; "Violet"; and "Ice Cream."

Publisher: Leah Huete de Maines
Editor: Christen Kincaid
Cover Art: Kathleen Raymond Roan
Author Photo: Carrie Matarese
Cover Design: Elizabeth Maines McCleavy

Order online: www.finishinglinepress.com
also available on amazon.com

Author inquiries and mail orders:
Finishing Line Press
PO Box 1626
Georgetown, Kentucky 40324
USA

Table of Contents

parable mood 1

Each of us has a different mother 2

Thread 3

Touch Here 4

Statue of Our Lady 5

Bearing Witness 6

Horse Farm 7

Prodigal 8

Reading Eavan Boland's 'That the Science of Cartography
    Is Limited' 9

Prescription 10

Tuft 11

Inheritance 12

Five Breaths 13

A Healer, Who 14

Japanese Town Fills Itself with Dolls 16

Mother Chooses to End Her Life by Fasting 17

Disappearance 18

Oh ye 19

Credo 20

Footprint 21

Among Chickens 22

Ice Cream 23

Violet 24

Mothers and Earth 25

Body Continuous 26

Notes 27

for my sisters, with love

parable mood

One day I said to a dead tree, *fall down*,
and it crashed at my feet. I called out
to the rest of the trees, those in groups
and those that came to take the place
of the dead tree, *fall!* And they fell too.
I turned to the lake, *dry up*, and it shrank,
draining into a hole until the lake-bottom
appeared like a derelict planet. The sun
would not stop heating the new land, so I said,
cover yourself, and it magnificently blew out.
Then the atmosphere crinkled into infinitesimal
folds and collapsed like shattered glass.
In the dark I could hear animals shifting
in panic, but only for a short while.
I rested, beyond time, beyond suffering,
until a thought arose. If I have such power,
to take life and take that which gives life,
perhaps I am master enough to create it.
But in the void I could not find my body
or a place to begin, or anyone to ask.

Each of us has a different mother

To my dark-haired sister she is
a first nun, mother superior.
To my curly-haired sister, a Juris Doctor,
mean-smart. To my third
and short-haired sister, a harmless
pigeon-woman, sweet, generous, pitiable.

I cradle her worn hand. Therein
a dwelling, the great indoors,
a ceiling and a floor, once
the triumphal arch between them,
twice a frightened woman, always
a woman's haste.

Now, she has forgotten what happened
earlier today, forgets lunch, to wash,
to give a fig about Christmas,
yet does not mistake us
for the fourth sister, the one we lost,
you can see it in her eyes.

Thread

With her smooth-edged index fingernail
and calloused thumb, my grandmother picked
invisible threads from the hem of my uniform skirt,
dropped them in a tiny pile
then passed a longer thread through a needle,
stabbed and pulled a wide tacking stitch,
finger joints swollen like newel post knobs.
Although she lived one thousand miles away
she was faintly annoyed without a chore to do.
My mother, now her age, did not learn to sew.
Today I woke her from her nap, asked
how she slept. *Did I nap?* she said while perched
on the side of the bed, *I don't remember. Oh
I'm thinking about Bernie, about everything,*
then looked past the top of my head into space.
I will take her to Hoffman's Nursery,
she'll thread her walker between the wooden planks
bowed with annual flats wide as stripes
in a victory flag, pull up beside the pump
and with help turn around in the gravel aisle.
When I lean down to adjust the brakes, she'll
twine her arms around my neck,
relieved to feel a texture she recalls.

Touch Here

After surgery a strange nurse
touches my feet and I wake
in a gray bathroom, every other tile
1960s mauve. My mother leans there,
forehead pressed to doorframe.
Beyond the door—a pale blue room.
In that room—royal blue spread.
A crowd of women, forest of legs,
press into a line from her side
of the bed through trees to cliff, sea.
Mother, here you are, here am I.
And they, too many to be named.
You wait, you have waited, will wait
but not for me. I am here.

Statue of Our Lady

Where to place her?

I circle the house
as if holding a winning lottery ticket,

her presence, an ocean liner afloat in air,
will-and-testament hull
filled with silver, disordered bars.

I am bemused by sums.

So many were named Mary,
teachers, classmates, my mother
Mary who prayed to Mary and for her,
passing the blessed icon
from child to child.

She has not let me sleep.

Warmth in my ear
as if mother and daughter embrace:

>   *Set her among the hellebores.*

Rain pools in her palm, stains
cement robes.

Bearing Witness

Anna Swir resisted the urge
      to eat paint, dive
from a third story, but not
      to hit her head
against her father's studio wall,
      carve her arms.
Yet she survived
      in spite of the body's
fluids and intrusions,
      parents degraded and mad
and still loving her, neighbors
      picked off by snipers,
their children, fat bellied
      with malnourishment,
locked in cupboards.
      Her hunger's source
could not be latched—
      such pain, such necessity—
as she opened her mouth
      to the taste
of continuous rain.

Horse Farm

Because I had seen them that day and she hadn't,
my sisters and I loaded her walker into the trunk
and drove down the lane to the quiet farm,
pulled off in the lot where Cora the goat had been tied.
But the horses were pastured, stalls open, empty.
So she, slower than melting ice, one foot forward,
the other held up a moment as if about to step back,
rolled with us close to her side. The horses, deep
in the meadow, did not look up when she waved
her hands by her throat and, panting, turned and dropped
on the walker's seat to rest in the silent late-day road.
I stayed while one sister, concerned, walked back
to the car and the other, annoyed, went with her,
lingered long enough to see at first a black, then roan,
then two black, two roan and a dapple, move across
deep tufted fields to the bottom pasture and out of sight.
We watched them follow each other at intervals
a few minutes apart as if slyly aware of something
they might not get to see, perhaps thirsty, but seeming
to hide their need to be like the others, looking up awhile,
then walking, a trot, soft gallop, paces the same
from our distance, as was the smooth light on their backs—
each the first to imagine a deeper shade and go.

Prodigal

She calls me in a rush
though she has nowhere to go,
as if words
might turn their back,
repudiate.
      Did he want to come live with you?
      I ask.
Yes, well no, not really,
he said he'd nowhere to go.
      He asked for money, right?
No, well yes, but I told him he couldn't have any.
He was surprised, said he hoped
I might have changed
since Bernie's death.
      Never give him money—
Why are you so stern—
I called to tell you I told him to call you
and two other things,
to go to the doctor
and one other thing.
      What was that?
Well, I expect him to do all three
things. I want you to be kind.
Why are you unkind—
He said you cut him off.
      That's not true.
Honey, he said it was.

Reading Eavan Boland's "That the Science of Cartography Is Limited"

Wherein a woman recollects
a woodland near Connacht.
She and her lover slow
to orient their passing
to a tremor in the scruffy grass,
and know they've stalled, at peace,
where forebears worked and died—
bleeding, bare-headed,
despairing, and with child—
stub of a famine road.
I too was born from buried labor,
excursions shadow-thin—
my mother's great grandmother
took an unmarked path through Clare
in that century's second famine's cresting wave,
across stone hills, cold as smooth-backed whales,
sub-strata where soil blew west
with nothing west but water,
past sodden sheds—she paused, looked in—
and onto Cork's lined piers,
up a plank to the stern
where she leaned so long watching
gravel shores gray and drown,
we have lost sight of her.

Prescription

Don't worry, he is still there beneath a textured sky,
seated in the filtered shade of an Australian pine.

Don't, although you are too far to hear him if he calls,
or detect the dry raking of those boughs.

You are alone, but only as you were the mornings
he watched you swim from up the beach,

you kicked your feet and tipped your head
all the way back until you could see his hat.

Now you must bite into your slice of sun
the way you would into an orange

and look up, though neck vertebrae crackle
like shards on the sea floor.

Do as the physical therapist has taught you.
Move arms in small circles taking deeper breaths,

feel your ankles strengthening. Every morning
cut an orange, then roll your walker back to the recliner

opposite his empty chair. Forgetful of everything,
enjoy it while he waits.

Tuft
for Mary Holdip

Red birds scatter off your mountain island
when you land in a broad-winged 707, stand
in our edgeless driveway, first snow.
At six, I am pure bluish yellow as this memory:
you staggering in the uncanny cold
eager for amazement, your warm weather microbes
ready to become eighty percent our own.
Snowfall with opened eyes, snow on my cheek
like the back of your hand, your prayers
also without edges, staying colorless, blind
through the hardest years. At ninety
your flat palms gather those tufts of grief,
keep them from falling, your voice still
runs water, calls. Our names in your dialect
are washed and dressed, softer, smaller.

Inheritance

When mother turned seventy, she moved
to a one-story house with a concrete skirt.
She wept when the black locust's bark
claimed her husband's face, his finger scolded.

Once, tugging the blinds, she fell and spent
the night enrapt in the ceiling fixture.
Its humming grew louder and finally burst
at the back of her eye. The tree was removed.

Soon she said the bearded man came in
and touched her gems. Rabbits counted
to ten in the valance, snakes filled
the commode. She hid canned goods.

I have come to her house with no trees
and a concrete skirt. I spend my days looking
for cash and the Con Ed stock in my name.
As I crawl towards the walls they collapse.

My mother said my legs are hickory trunks.
Now they straddle the constant pulse of frogs
and an airy darkness. As I grope for right angles
to make a home, her voice rebukes.

Five Breaths

You hold the fish-bone shoulders in a way that was ever impossible,
the shape feels vaguely impious.
You were always the one to cry first.
Now your tears soak chin and neck, the slot between your breasts.

Your siblings stand backs to the wall, none will approach the bed,
you turn her hairless head, open
the drying mouth, brush your hands
on your legs, the feel of her face, its smooth skin-smear flakes.

The shape of her breath is unnatural, soil gouged by a plow,
thrown up by an underground pest.
It rises sharply then sharply falls
yet is still emphatic, as if she would call you a whore, call you hideous.

But these are the last five breaths with long spaces between them,
and its Sunday here at the hospice.
You hold your breath while the room ticks.
You look up for the first to move. In this version no one moves.

A Healer, Who

and your daughters shall prophecy
and your old men shall dream dreams
Acts 2

First

Each morning she shuts
the door to the prayer room,
drops slowly to the deep-armed chair,
opens the book on the music stand
to the marked page, hears
the underlined words
in her father's voice: so that
> *they should set their hope in He*
> *who cleft rock in the wilderness,*
> *caused streams*
> *to flow down like rivers,*
hears his last words again
as the wind blew warm
through the windowless house:
> *Do not forget*
and she wedged her childish soul
beneath his narrow bed,
carefully turned on her back.
> *I am well, all is well.*

She had seen a flame cascading,
watched it enter his head.

Second

At her 90th birthday party there are many tables.
One member of each family rises in succession, approaches.
Bent forward on her cane, she listens—
She had washed their dying mother, braided the hair
of a wayward child, coaxed a gun from my father's grip
with kindling words, re-named us when we were young.

Yet today, Monday, during our call, she says she can't see
herself in those stories any more than she does in windows
alive with glass saints, and such honors waste breath
as baskets of flowers for the dead waste money for bread.
Hold the law in a rebellious heart, she says and laughs,
and wash yourself each day in the baptismal fire.

Third

She cups the back of my childish head,
smooths tawny hair, tugs. A rough
cloth down shiny legs, sweet water
soaped on the back. Her palm
warms my forehead, cheek, neck.
Lifted onto the counter, I cool.
Over and over, lifted.

Japanese Town Fills Itself with Dolls

Scent of cedar
from our lush valley
settles on yarn hair—
how good it smells.
Your cotton cheek,
cool as rain-washed
stepping stones.
Pollen drifting
from Mountain Ash
stains my arms
as I carry you
like a flower-offering
and lay you against
the broad trunk. Mud
on your corduroy seat
and knees, the short
jacket you wore
in the last festival.
Forgive me
for doing and undoing
your bone buttons.
I have lingered
long in order to bear
your silence, hear joy
bubbling beneath sorrow—
spring thaw.
How I have missed
your laughter.

Mother Chooses to End Her Life by Fasting

And daughter agrees to film it
for all our sakes, those who might someday
wish to choose a similar path.
And Rosemary, child of the 1930s,
who would never become a burden,
who stayed in a motel when visiting family,
did her own shopping at ninety-four,
finally accepts assistance.
The hospice has let her in though, you see,
she has no fatal disease.
Now, having swallowed a last bit of crab cake, sip of tea,
having called her children, grand-children and few
remaining friends, she lies back on the aqua pillow and waits.
Then, it's the fourth day.
Pain is receding, she says, hunger abating, body
lifting, at peace, she smiles, fulfilling
a long-held wish to die in her own way.
Then, late on the seventh day,
she says to her daughter,
>*honey, you look hungry,*
>*go eat something,*

and, Mary, link to our common soul,
who will stay to the very end, stumbles
to the parking lot, bursts into tears.

Disappearance
for E. P.

as his memory thins
he fades, transparencing
through a table on his way to falling
my *love*, your brilliance
and the redwood's smoldering
holy towers, prone
cover my face
the firefighter's bulky silhouette
and burning eyes
North Complex, Slater, Creek, Campfire in paradise
loss in bone deep waterless
Venusian bursts
eruption: veneriad
planet without topography or
spheres to see with, shapes earned
inflamed retina
I call him *love* and he looks
through me

Oh ye

He said, *go,* he needed to pray alone,
I will meet you on the other side,
then disappeared into desert haze,
rough robe wavy at the hem
as if catching a light breeze before vanishing.
And they rose from flat rocks, lifted
mended nets, walked with faces turned
toward the red-black sea.

I have seen such trouble forecast,
watched the horizon all week,
told my parents *go, get out of there*
while the sea rose solid as a temple wall
and yachts were tossed across Main Street,
fishing sheds, street signs, trucks
plunged in oily water.

But they would not leave,
my beloveds.

They climbed on a stool,
then the counter, up the open shelves
as water burst their bungalow door
and fire flickered through shiny weeds.
Mother, sucked by an undertow
until he could hold her no longer.
Father, wedged in an awning window
after diving for her, down, down.

What more is required to see a dolphin
in a wave riding in and on the trackless water,
>   see
>   beyond fear,
take up table legs, plastic pallets,
and pass over the deep like disciples?

Let me hold you within my storm's eye,
all of us, eternally, someone's child.

Credo

Feel the invisible back-body where the attention dwells
in a room lined with faithful lying supine.

Feel the front-facing arrangement of eyes
in a flash of half-perception made whole.

Feel the front body, familiar as an elementary school
never entered that way except on Sundays and Holy Days

when we filtered beneath its wooden portico, across
a flagstone terrace, through wide-winged glass doors.

Feel its heartbeat, a scuffed gymnasium, often sanctuary
for Word and Eucharist, sometimes a parish hall or cafeteria—

deafening at noon—once a theater where eighth-grade
English watched *Lord Jim,* heard hushed footsteps backstage,

and in whose purring chest my parents rise clumsily
from folding chairs, throats unwinding in ensemble

    I believe in one God

visible and invisible, in heaven and on earth, true
and as uncertain, yet somehow, for me, a refuge in so saying.

Footprint
> *for Anna Maria Leitgeb*

I wish we could stay as we are.
Lawn chairs in the driveway,
February sun, legs outstretched
and ankles crossed as if in Salten-Schlern,
the children sliding down the low
mountain pushed up by the plow.
We watch while turned towards
each other, follow peaked caps
and bundled arms, hoots and screams—
our souls at play in the brilliance.
You write in a language I don't speak,
long for a language I can't hear,
and somehow, as long as we stay
side by side, I long for it too. First
with the sound of your father's axe,
then your mother's song, distant,
wistful, then our shadowed prints
smaller and smaller up the valley.

Among Chickens

A hill outside Penn Yan slopes up from flat
onion fields, long winding rows upturned,
alive with flatbed trucks. I've stopped
to feed the chickens penned on Sophie's farm,
watch them zigzag in a group, run to the gate
with leaping steps and stop, mesmerized,
their faint, mewling chatter silenced.
They are simple and short-lived, and I am
like a god, welcomed, warmly pressed
to ruffled bodies, purple, copper spangled,
green, swift as black-eyed minnows, seasonal
as leaves. I raise the dented feeding tray,
all heads turn up. Above us, silvered sky.

Ice Cream

If she falls we won't be able to lift her,
my sister worries as our mother
staggers around the kitchen island
gripping the counter's edge. We urge
her to straighten up, stop tipping forward,
balance evenly on her feet. And she does,
a little, stopping often to look around
as if the steepness in the house
is unfamiliar, creeps back to the recliner,
exhausted. She stares into the midground
and I ask what she is thinking about
and she says *ice cream*, then falls asleep.
Tall vanilla soft-serve from one
of the first machines in California,
smooth-sweet, cool, like nothing else,
nothing at all, while swaying on the wide
couch-seat of grandpa's Buick
as he makes his weekly vendor's rounds.
The car rolls to a stop, windows down,
lime tree blossoms on pine-dry air.
He tucks his hands beneath her arms,
lifts gently. She has fallen asleep.

Violet

I stole it from the sill above my mother's sink
when she was in the hospital last year, a gift
from one of my sisters or step-sisters or step-
sisters-in-law, loose in its Dixie cup of soil, hairy
leaves blackening at the edges and dusty, barely
hanging on that lonely precipice. Yes, among
our women, doing good may not be secret virtue
but watered down with shame. Today, after solid
weeks of sky a cathedral ceiling tarped with gray,
typical for our town so near the lake, sun shines
on it, and on my back as I turn from the window
and let my ribs warm. Solid purple blossoms
with egg-yolk yellow hearts. I'll take a picture
and send it to my youngest sister, ask forgiveness.
Mother has been home a while, has she not noticed?
So not into plants, all greenery, lots of green things
she would say. Tell her, if she asks, it blossoms
and we are warm, as water, as stone.

Mothers and Earth

When I drive South after six weeks
away, I notice she struggles to listen
to news of my family, my work, scenes
from the lake where I live. She slips

as well in the urge to hear, content
to get it partly right, tumbles into a doze
when I stand, sleeps between puzzles, calls,
meals, and now, at times, declines

with a shrug to go to the table. Yet she's glad
I'm here. A woman with hundreds of friends,
endlessly chatting, endlessly busy
with projects, plans. Now there's less thinking.

Not that she's dim, she is bright. Something
outside her is shedding less light. Home,
I walk up the hill through the woodland's
patterned declivities, golden soil,

pods of migrating dark-eyed souls.
The rustling woods are unusually quiet.

Yet it still smells right, our earth, and appears
contented with fewer attractions, wheeling
toward darkness from which it arose, as if
this is what nature intended, to leave me.

Body Continuous

I love the humpback's song,
her care for her young taught to find food
in the surf through play, and later
in bubble nets on Stellwagen Bank.
I love her ungendered names:
Salt, Spinaker, Lune,
primacy etched in flukes' markings,
family tree held closely
by scientists and detanglers, private
as her positions in and through the Gulf of Maine.
I love whale-people who watch obsessively from Race Point,
converse without moving their glasses
off the horizon, read plumes, record each sighting.
I long to know whale-effort,
an instant of one trillionth of her mass,
but fear my love is rather love for those whose love is effort.
Massive head, crusty skin and razor-fine baleen plate,
fins like wings for navigation, pole to pole,
are not these legs, weighted heart, so seized
as if each inch of flesh is solid as the planet.
She is outside myself.
But here, in the shallows, I sense a ghost-track
hiding the unforeseen, magnetic pairing,
current's ease, body continuous.

Notes

"Bearing Witness" was inspired by Anna Swir's stunning collection *Talking to My Body*, Copper Canyon Press, 1996, translated by Czeslaw Milosz and Leonard Nathan.

Eavan Boland's beautiful poem can be found in *In a Time of Violence*, W.W. Norton, 1994.

"A Healer, Who" The words quoted by the character's father are from Psalm 78.

"Oh ye" The reference in stanza one is to John 6:15—16, a scene also depicted in the books of Matthew and Mark.

"Japanese Town Fills Itself with Dolls" was written in response to an article in the New York Times that touches on the powerful need to love, to mother, even when there are no children to be found: https://www.nytimes.com/2019/12/17/world/asia/japan-dolls-shrinking-population.

"Mother Chooses to End Her Life by Fasting" was in response to an article in the Washington Post that moved me deeply: https://www.washingtonpost.com/local/social-issues/at-94-she-was-ready-to-die-by-fasting-her-daughter-filmed-it/2019/11/03/41688230-fcd9-11e9-8190-6be4deb56e01_story.html

"Body Continuous" was inspired by the dedicated whale watchers at the tip of Cape Cod and at Point Vincente in Rancho Palos Verdes, Los Angeles County.

Victoria Korth is a practicing psychiatrist caring for the chronically mentally ill. Her poem "Harlem Valley Psychiatric Center" won the 2020 Montreal International Poetry Prize. Poems have appeared in *Jelly Bucket, Broad River Review, Ocean State Review, Tar River Poetry, LEON Literary Review,* as well as *Spoon River Poetry Review, Barrow Street* and widely elsewhere. Her chapbook, *Cord Color,* was released from Finishing Line Press in 2015. She is an MFA graduate of the Warren Wilson College Program for Writers and holds an MA in English/Creative Writing from SUNY Brockport.

www.ingramcontent.com/pod-product-compliance
Lightning Source LLC
LaVergne TN
LVHW041513070426
835507LV00012B/1547